ISBN: 979-8-9944348-0-2
Printed in the United States

Library of Congress Control Number: 2026900022

Scripture quotations are taken from the Holy Bible, New Living
Translation, copyright ©1996, 2004, 2015 by Tyndale House Foundation.
Used by permission of Tyndale House Publishers, Carol Stream, Illinois
60188. All rights reserved.

Illustrated By: Jennifer Kain

BROKEN YET BELOVED
A 30 DAY DEVOTIONAL FOR WOMEN
LIVING WITH CHRONIC ILLNESS

BY JENNIFER KAIN

DEDICATED TO EVERY WOMAN WHO IS BATTLING AN INVISIBLE WAR THAT NOBODY CAN SEE. YOU ARE ALWAYS SEEN BY GOD.

TABLE OF CONTENTS

Week 1: God Is With Me in This

Theme Verse: "The Lord is close to the brokenhearted;
he rescues those whose spirits are crushed."
—Psalm 34:18 NLT

Day 1

Thereafter, Hagar used another name to refer to the LORD, who had spoken to her. She said, "You are the God who sees me." She also said, "Have I truly seen the One who sees me?"

— Gen 16:13 NLT

Reflection

You don't have to explain yourself to God. He already sees. Hagar wasn't just overlooked. She was mistreated, cast aside, and forgotten by the people who should have protected her. Maybe that feels familiar. When your pain doesn't show up on scans, when your fatigue is mistaken for laziness, when your grief is minimized. It's easy to feel invisible.

But there, in the desert, when everything had run out, Hagar encountered the God who saw her fully. She didn't have to convince Him that her suffering was real. She didn't have to advocate or justify. She was simply seen.

God sees you, too. Not just the version you put together for others, but the true you, fighting through flare-ups, canceling plans again, trying to smile when you feel like crumbling.

He sees your invisible battles. He knows the hours you spend recovering in silence. He hears the prayers you whisper through clenched teeth. He counts your tears like treasure.

You are not forgotten. You are not faking. You are not too much. You are fully seen by the One who matters most.

God is the God of seeing. Even when you feel forgotten, you are not alone. Often, when we go places or use a handicap placard, people don't see what you feel. They judge what they don't understand. Know that God sees you every minute of every day.

Prayer

Lord, thank You for being the God who sees me. When I feel dismissed or misunderstood, remind me that You know my heart and my body better than anyone. Help me find peace in Your presence today. Amen.

Prompt

When have you felt unseen or misunderstood because of your illness? How might it change things to know that God sees it all?

Thoughts

Day 2
The God Who Knows Pain

He was despised and rejected—a man of sorrows, acquainted with deepest grief. We turned our backs on him and looked the other way. He was despised, and we did not care.

—Isaiah 53:3 NLT

Reflection

Jesus knows chronic pain. Not just theoretically, but intimately. He didn't float through life untouched by human experience. He felt fatigue, hunger, rejection, and grief. He knew what it meant to be misunderstood, doubted, and even mocked for who He was. The weight of emotional and physical pain didn't escape Him. For those living with invisible conditions, this matters. When people question your symptoms or dismiss your reality, you can cling to a Savior who doesn't. Jesus gets it. He was called crazy by His own family. He was judged for how He lived. He carried deep sorrow, like the ache you carry. And because of this, you never suffer alone. Your pain has a companion. Your long nights have a witness. Your body may be failing in ways others can't see, but Jesus sees, and He feels it alongside you. He is not only your Savior. He is your fellow sufferer, your strength, and your safe place.

After a long day of hiking through the Arizona wilderness, my legs were exhausted and I could barely walk another step. The next day was work, and I had to use my cane to keep upright from the pain. Coworkers asked if something had happened or quietly stared without making eye contact. It weighs on you when you have a dynamic disability. One day, you look like nothing is wrong, and the next, you can barely move. It's in the unpredictability that I call out to the Lord for help and strength. It's the strength to ignore the judgments and the socially awkward stares. You don't have to justify to anyone why you need a mobility device. It's not their business unless you want to share. God knows what's going on, and some days that's enough.

Prayer

Jesus, thank You for knowing pain and walking this road with me. Help me remember that I'm never alone in my suffering. Let Your presence be my comfort. Amen.

Prompt

Where in your body or life do you feel pain right now? What does it mean to you that Jesus is "familiar with suffering"?

Thoughts

Day 3
My Body is Not a Burden

Thank you for making me so wonderfully complex! Your workmanship is marvelous how well I know it.

—Psalm 139:14 NLT

Reflection

Some days, your body feels like the enemy. It limits you, betrays you, and embarrasses you. You may wonder, How could this be "wonderfully made"? But the truth of Scripture doesn't change when your body does. God's craftsmanship includes your nervous system, your mitochondria, your joints, and yes, even the parts that ache or don't work the way they should. You are not broken because you are ill. You are broken and beautiful. You are beloved and weary. God doesn't see your condition as a flaw in His design. He sees it as part of your sacred story. When you feel like a burden to your family, to society, even to yourself, God says you are worthy. Not for what you can do, but because of who you are: His.

I found that I wrestled with this verse after I was diagnosed with my condition of Hypermobile Ehlers-Danlos Syndrome. It's about reframing everything. Your day used to consist of endless to-do lists. Now it's about making a list, getting to everything you can, and not feeling bad about the things you didn't get to. Don't let the guilt get in the way of living your best life. While it's hard to believe that God would let your body become the way it has, don't think for a moment He isn't redeeming you through it.

Prayer

God, help me believe I am wonderfully made, even when my body feels like it's falling apart. Remind me that I am not a burden, I am Your beloved. Amen.

Prompt

What part of your body have you seen as a burden? How can you speak truth over it today?

Thoughts

Day 4
Invisible Doesn't Mean Imaginary

So we don't look at the troubles we can see now; rather, we fix our gaze on things that cannot be seen. For the things we see now will soon be gone, but the things we cannot see will last forever.

—2 Corinthians 4:18 NLT

Reflection

Living with an invisible illness can feel like gaslighting. You know something is wrong. You feel it constantly. And yet others doubt it, or worse, suggest it's "in your head." But God never asks you to prove your pain. Scripture is full of the unseen realities of our faith, such as love, hope, and eternity. Our hope is in a Heaven that can't be seen. What we have is more sacred. You don't need external validation to be believed by God. Your symptoms are real. Your suffering is valid. Your experience matters. God sees what others can't. He's not waiting for test results to confirm what He already knows.

When I was younger, the Spirit spoke to me. He said to me that one day, when you are older, something will happen and you're whole life will change. It's an odd thing to be told when you're a new Christian at 11 years old, but the more I read the Bible, the more I knew this was true. Something big would happen, but of course, I also thought something awful would transpire. What I didn't know was that getting this diagnosis would be the thing that changed my life for the better. Now I'm not saying that having an invisible illness hasn't come with challenges, but God knew I needed to be reassured long ago that if it's in His will, then why do you have to worry? This illness has taken me to places and people I would've never met otherwise, and my life is so much richer because of it.

Prayer

Lord, thank You for being the God who sees the invisible. Help me anchor my worth in Your truth, not others' opinions. Let me feel peace knowing that You believe me. Amen.

Prompt

Write down 3 things others can't see about your illness, but God does.

Thoughts

Day 5
When You're Dismissed or Misunderstood

Then they sat on the ground with him for seven days and nights. No one said a word to Job, for they saw that his suffering was too great for words.

—Job 2:13 NLT

Reflection

Job's friends did something right, at first. They simply sat with him. No lectures. No advice. Just presence. When you live with invisible pain, people often rush to fix or explain you. "Have you tried yoga?" "At least it's not cancer." "You don't look sick." And though some mean well, those words can deepen the hurt. What you need is not a cure-all. It's a companion. Someone to sit with you, acknowledge your reality, and stay. God offers that. His Spirit is not quick to judge or fix. He abides. And though people may fail to understand, you are still worth understanding. Your story is still holy ground.

There are a few books that discuss how Christians with disabilities have been treated within the Church. Those references will be at the back of this book. I had a hard time explaining my condition to anyone in the church because on the toughest of days, when the pain was big, I wanted someone to sit with me and tell me they loved me and they were willing to listen. I never wanted someone to "fix" me. Although I'm sure many of you reading this have all had someone "pray" for your healing from your illness. After a while, I had to distance myself from the "healing fix" that people got from praying. If someone does that to you in the future, consider what is happening in their heart and pray for them. What outcome do they need to feel?

Maybe they are praying for you because they genuinely care, but often they are misguided in thinking that this time you will be healed. When in reality, the only one who can heal is God. I firmly believe I was meant to get sick, but that doesn't mean I haven't asked God to take this pain away, so I can get back to "my life". For me, this was the wrong approach. EDS (which is what is short-hand for Ehlers-Danlos Syndrome) is not a quick fix. It's a genetic condition that affects every aspect of your body and its function.

I hope you find and surround yourself with a community that understands you and your limitations. That asks questions to understand and is patient to listen. We need more listeners from our able-bodied Christians than judgment and "fixing".

Prayer

God, when I feel dismissed or minimized, be my comfort. Help me find people who can sit with me like Job's friends did without fixing or judging. Help me be that person for others too. Amen.

Prompt

What would it look like to allow someone to sit with your pain without fixing it? Who might be safe enough to try?

Thoughts

Day 6
Naming the Ache

I am worn out from sobbing. All night I flood my bed with weeping, drenching it with my tears.

—Psalm 6:6 NLT

Reflection

Naming your pain isn't weakness, it's worship. The psalmists cried out without filtering their emotions. They said things like "How long, O Lord?" and "Why have You forsaken me?" and God didn't rebuke them. He preserved their words in Scripture. You don't need to hide your true feelings behind a spiritual smile. God can handle your doubt, your anger, your despair. He invites it. Naming the ache lets light in. It allows God to meet you in the raw places. So say it. Write it. Whisper it. Cry it out. The Lord is listening, and He will not turn away.

Pain doesn't have to be physical; it can also be mental. Choosing to acknowledge this can bring acceptance and understanding. When all you feel is isolation, it's easy to think nobody understands your pain, but your Creator does. When I engage in activities that involve movement, my knees always seem to remind me that they are weak and tired, but I acknowledge that pain, so I can help soothe them. I am reminded that God hears my prayers to soothe the pain I can't fix. It is frustrating when I can't find a quick solution.

My knees have been a particular point of issue because they're the first part of my body where I realized I needed help. My knees needed a mobility aid. A few summers ago, I was in conversation with a few good friends, sitting at the kitchen table, and I finally asked about my desire to use a cane, but it terrified me. My friend told me not to be ashamed of using a mobility aid. If it helps conserve energy and improve weight distribution, I should try it. I don't know why there's a stigma for someone who doesn't look a "certain age" to use a cane. Marketing does a good job of making anyone who isn't the proper age feel bad about using mobility aids. In the end, I'm glad I embraced the advice because now I use mobility aides all the time. Dynamic disabilities are hard to navigate. There's no rulebook for how to live now that everything feels upside down. Remember, God hears your prayers.

Prayer

God, I name my ache today. I lay it before You. Raw and unedited. Thank You for being a safe place for every emotion I carry. Amen.

Prompt

Write out your version of a lament psalm. Begin with "How long, O Lord..." and be honest.

Thoughts

Day 7

God's Eye is on the Hidden Ones

The Lord is close to the brokenhearted;
he rescues those whose spirits are crushed.

—Psalm 38:18 NLT

Reflection

You don't have to be center-stage to be the center of God's heart. In a world obsessed with productivity, visibility, and "hustle," your stillness can feel like irrelevance. However, God often works in quiet ways. He draws near in the invisible spaces, in hospital beds, in tear-streaked pillows, in lonely afternoons.

If you are brokenhearted, God is near. If your spirit is crushed, He's already at your side. That's not poetry, it's a promise. You are not forgotten. You are not disqualified. You are the very one God draws near to.

At times when I am a part of a large group of people at work, it's hard not to feel like I'm the only one in the room who has a chronic illness. People will unintentionally create things that they think are great for the whole group, but which won't work for you in the slightest. It's easy to get angry and feel slighted. Getting quiet and listening to God can be one of the most powerful things to do in that moment. Constantly having to navigate a world that doesn't accommodate makes me feel like I'm on an island. It can be as simple as asking for clarity on the decision being made or sharing why the action makes you feel excluded or unconsidered. It is easy to be angry in those moments.

God wants to show you in those moments, when you stay angry, that it's not someone's intention to get it wrong, even if it feels that way. I have found this to be true in group settings when food is involved. As someone with a chronic illness, I have to eat a special set of things to not upset my ecosystem. It's probably the same for you. I feel for you, and I hope you eventually find a group of people who care and can accommodate your diet. When I feel powerless to change the situation, I am reminded that God wants me to be in that group event or meeting for a reason. You're a blessing to those around you, even if you can't eat the food. At times, it's exhausting to constantly have to bring your own food to things, but after a while, you get used to it. I'm in the still getting used to it phase.

Becoming chronically ill and disabled can happen at any age. On average, it takes someone 21 days to form a habit, but when it comes to irregular things in life, it can take much longer. For me, I've realized sitting in my anger doesn't do anyone good. My mental health takes a dive, and I am not in a good place. When you focus on the good of an event you want to be at and all the benefits it offers, the other inconveniences seem small in comparison. The world isn't made for us, and adjusting to it takes time. The Lord is close to you in your trials. Even if they seem small, it matters to our Creator.

Prayer

Lord, thank You that Your nearness doesn't depend on my strength. Be close to me today in my weakness. Let me feel the tenderness of Your presence. Amen.

Prompt

What does "God is close" mean to you personally today?

Thoughts

Week 2 Strength in Stillness

Theme Verse: "Be still, and know that I am God!"
—Psalm 46:10a (NLT)

When your body forces you to slow down, God meets you in the stillness.

Day 8

Radical Rest

He lets me rest in green meadows;
he leads me beside peaceful streams.

—Psalm 23:2 NLT

Reflection

When chronic illness brings your life to a halt, it can feel like you've been pushed to the sidelines. Everything you thought you'd do today, or this year, feels out of reach. However, the truth of Psalm 23 reminds us that God Himself sometimes allows the rest. This isn't weakness; it's a holy pause. God meets you in the green meadow you never planned to visit. The peace He offers doesn't come from productivity, but from His presence.

In most modern cultures, it's all about the hustle. It took time to learn how to stop. While it's not easy to do all the time, I've stopped caring about what others think or how slowly I walk to get places. The Phoenix sun in the summer can make even stepping outside a nightmare, and I have to do these things. I can't stay in for three months and watch the world go by when it's the hottest time of the year. Embracing these moments and taking actions like hydrating or using a mobility device when it's difficult are essential in new situations.

Rest looks different when managing chronic illness. At times, it feels like walking through your neighborhood, or like finding joy lying on the couch. I get frustrated when I can't do what I want. Do you ever have that feeling? Letting go of control is challenging. When God is in control, all things work according to His plans, not yours.

The question you have to ask yourself is this: Is it worth pushing through? Who are you impressing? Are you worried you're taking yet another sick day? These are all questions I ask myself every time I am forced to stop and pause. At some point on this journey, I decided to give God control and let divine rest wash over me. Now, this doesn't mean I'll be better in a day or even in a week, but what I do know is that this time God won.

Consider this prayer to meditate on in your prayer time

8 Then Jesus said, "Come to me, all of you who are weary and carry heavy burdens, and I will give you rest. 29 Take my yoke upon you. Let me teach you, because I am humble and gentle at heart, and you will find rest for your souls. 30 For my yoke is easy to bear, and the burden I give you is light."
Matthew 11:28–30 NLT

Prayer

Jesus, help me to receive this rest as an invitation, not as punishment. Quiet my anxious thoughts and meet me in this stillness with Your peace.

Prompt

How might your view of rest shift if you believed it was a gift from God, not a failure?

Thoughts

Day 9
The Gift of Slowness

So we don't look at the troubles we can see now;
rather, we fix our gaze on things that cannot be seen.

- 2 Corinthians 4:18 NLT

Reflection

When your body forces you to live at half-speed, you notice things others rush past. This slowness can open your eyes to what's eternal: unseen love, compassion, and grace. What if your chronic condition isn't taking you out of life, but deeper into it? Paul reminds us that what's seen is temporary, but what's unseen is everlasting. Sometimes slowness isn't a loss, it's a shift in vision.

It's when you get acutely sick or have a bad flare-up that you remember the God who loves and cares for you. Or the people in your life that come close when you need your basic things done, like laundry or making you dinner. Getting this type of sick often isn't a sign of progress, but one of exasperation. There are days when all I want to do with my free time is create and write, but a pounding headache or something else gets in the way of achieving my goal. It's in those moments you have to step back and thank God for the day you've been given. No matter how dull and awful it might be.

Lean into the gift of slowness. What is one thing you can achieve today if you are stuck with pain that has uninvitedly appeared? If you're anything like me, you want to do something that feels worthy of a day. Looking to God and reflecting on things you are grateful for can help with despair. I read once that the brain can't hold both anxiety and gratitude at the same time. You are so loved by the Lord. Let your day be led through His love.

Consider this prayer to meditate on in your prayer time

Give thanks to the Lord, for he is good! His faithful love endures forever.
1 Chronicles 16:34

Prayer

Lord, when I'm tempted to mourn all I can no longer do, help me notice what I now see more clearly. Let me fix my eyes on You.

Prompt

What "unseen" things have become more visible to you since your diagnosis or health decline?

Thoughts

Day 10
The Rest Jesus Offers

Then Jesus said, 'Come to me, all of you who are weary and carry heavy burdens, and I will give you rest.

—Matthew 11:28 NLT

Reflection

Jesus never shamed the weary. He welcomed them. When your body aches or your fatigue feels unrelenting, His words are not "try harder," but "come to Me." This rest isn't just physical, it's deep soul rest. The kind that tells you you're not defined by your pain, nor forgotten in it. His rest is healing, and it is freely given.

It's hard to define rest in the world of chronic illness. People say, "get some rest," as if we will be physically restored afterward. There are times when sleep works, and other times it doesn't. The type of rest the scripture speaks of is eternal, everlasting rest in the Father. When you pray to God, the Holy Spirit ripples over your soul. It feels like a reset.

A way I have found to rest in His spirit is to listen to worship music. When you're too tired for words, listening to others sing about Christ can help ease your fears and help you feel less alone.

Consider this prayer to meditate on in your prayer time

The rain and snow come down from the heavens
and stay on the ground to water the earth.
They cause the grain to grow,
producing seed for the farmer
and bread for the hungry.
11 It is the same with my word.
I send it out, and it always produces fruit.
It will accomplish all I want it to,
and it will prosper everywhere I send it.
12 You will live in joy and peace.
The mountains and hills will burst into song,
and the trees of the field will clap their hands!
-Isaiah 55:10-12 NLT

Prayer

Jesus, I come to You just as I am, tired, hurting, and unsure. Teach me to rest in Your love, not just for my body, but for my whole being.

Prompt

In what ways are you carrying burdens alone that Jesus has already offered to carry with you?

Thoughts

Day 11
Stillness Is Not Stagnation

The Lord himself will fight for you. Just stay calm.

—Exodus 14:14 NLT

Reflection

Stillness doesn't mean you're doing nothing; it means you're letting God do what only He can. Chronic illness can feel like life has passed you by, but even in the waiting, there is divine activity. While the Israelites panicked by the sea, God told them to be still, not because there was nothing to do, but because He was already doing it. You don't have to earn healing, provision, or peace. God is already moving on your behalf.

It's easy to forget that God is always working for you, besides you. In the good and bad times. When there's a new symptom or flare-up that lasts longer than expected, God knew and prepared you for it. Over the years, I have found that I draw closer to God when this happens. It's in his timing, not ours.

Consider this prayer to meditate on in your prayer time

16 Always be joyful. 17 Never stop praying. 18 Be thankful in all circumstances, for this is God's will for you who belong to Christ Jesus.
– 1 Thessalonians 5:16–18 NLT

Prayer

Father, when I feel stuck or stagnant, remind me that You are still fighting for me. Help me find peace in the pause.

Prompt

What if your stillness is not evidence of failure, but trust? What could that change for you?

Thoughts

Day 12
Rest as Resistance

The Lord himself will fight for you. Just stay calm.

—Psalm 127:2 NLT

Reflection

We live in a world that worships hustle. But when you live with chronic illness, rest isn't optional; it's survival. Psalm 127 calls overwork useless. That's radical grace. Rest becomes an act of spiritual resistance. It says: "I trust that God works even when I don't." Your worth is not measured by what you produce, but by how you live. In God's kingdom, rest is holy.

Ask yourself these questions: Do I love God? Do I trust God wants the best for me? Does God promise to finish the work he started in us?

If the answer to all of these questions is YES, then look at the rest as a way to honor God.

I had to learn how to rest well. Not stopping for five minutes, but resting for thirty. It's never convenient, but it's necessary to survive. If not, I get worse. It's difficult because I'm ambitious and I'm sure you are too, but resting is important to living with chronic illness.

There was a time when I would drive across town to be with a group of women who had chronic illnesses like mine, and our leader vented her frustration to us.

"I was so angry that I had to lie on the couch today, instead of preparing for group. All I did was some housework, and I got tired. God reminded me I needed to take a nap, so I wasn't exhausted for tonight," she told our small group. Her vulnerability made me realize we are not much different than one another. We might have different names for our illnesses, but fatigue is a common symptom across many of them. Who do you need to let in on your secret about how fatigue can crush you? While that person might not understand right away, if they care for you, they want to know how to support you in your time of exhaustion.

Prayer

God, I lay down my guilt and my striving. Let my rest be a declaration that I am already enough in Your eyes.

Prompt

How have you internalized the idea that rest is lazy or weak? What does God say instead?

Thoughts

Day 13
When You Can't Even Pray

And the Holy Spirit helps us in our weakness... when we don't know what God wants us to pray for, the Holy Spirit prays for us...

—Romans 8:26 NLT

Reflection

There are days when words won't come. Pain is too loud. Fatigue is too deep. But you are never left without an intercessor. Romans 8 tells us that the Holy Spirit prays for us, with groanings too deep for words. God understands the language of your sighs. You are never voiceless in the Kingdom of Heaven.

There are days I don't know what to pray, but I thank God for this moment. What I need to ask God is for Him to reveal his promises to me. I need to see the tangible love of His presence. Whether it's a cozy blanket or a good book. God can be seen in different ways.

When I was first diagnosed, I took it minute by minute and prayed God would show up. It's how I knew I needed to make a big change to my diet. I listened to the Holy Spirit, and gradually, the detoxing made me feel slightly better.

Praying doesn't always heal the body, but how is it changing you on the inside? How might we surrender to the moment and give it all to our creator? The grieving process of living in a body that constantly fails you is a humbling experience. God doesn't always heal your physical body, but gives a path forward to live in abundance and joy.

Prayer

Holy Spirit, thank You for praying when I can't. Help me trust that even in my silence, You hear everything I feel.

Prompt

Write down what you wish you could say to God today, even if it's messy or incomplete.

Thoughts

Day 14
Strength in the Quiet

This is what the Sovereign Lord says: Only in returning to me and resting in me will you be saved. In quietness and confidence is your strength

—Isaiah 30:15 NLT

Reflection

God does not demand noise or effort to draw near. In fact, Isaiah says that your strength is found in quietness and rest. That's countercultural. Your quiet life, your long pauses, your cancelled plans, your gentle pace, may actually be where your greatest strength is born. This week, let God rewrite your definition of strength.

I had to have an attitude adjustment when learning to rest. Getting upset was not going to get me anywhere. If you live with a partner, spouse, or roommate, it takes them time to understand what strength in rest looks like, too.

I don't know if you're like this, but I set high expectations of myself and what I can get done in a day. For years, I had an ongoing list of things I needed to accomplish daily in order to feel fulfilled, and when I got sick, that idealism died that day. Maybe, even a little part of myself died too. The overachieving perfectionist had to get cast aside, and I had to learn to be patient and appreciate what I could get done on my list. Now, there are days when this becomes an excuse, and that, my friend, is a hard line to walk, so be careful there. On the other side of the bridge, I've noticed how achieving less on my to-do list and asking for help has increased my joy in the day. Less stress helps everything in most cases. It's not about being perfect, but being an imperfect sinner trying to love God daily and repenting when your perfectionism gets the best of you.

Consider this prayer to meditate on in your prayer time

The Lord wants to show his mercy to you. He wants to rise and comfort you. The Lord is a fair God, and everyone who waits for his help will be happy.
—Isaiah 30:18 NLT

Prayer

God, thank You for not needing my performance. Let me find strength not in noise, but in Your gentle presence.

Prompt

Where have you seen strength emerge through stillness in your own journey?

Thoughts

Week 3 I Am Not My Diagnosis

Theme Verse: For we are God's masterpiece. He has created
us anew in Christ Jesus..."
—Ephesians 2:10a NLT

Your diagnosis may explain your condition, but it does not define your worth.

Day 15
More Than a Label

Anyone who belongs to Christ has become a new person. The old life is gone; a new life has begun!

—2 Corinthians 5:17 NLT

Reflection

When your symptoms become daily companions, it's easy to feel like they define you. But you are not your diagnosis. You are not a list of limitations. You are a new creation in Christ. Illness might change what your days look like, but it doesn't erase who you are. God sees all of you, your strength, your story, and your soul, and calls you His.

When you remember who you were before getting sick, what do you see? Are those things still true today? Or did they shift? I found, reminding myself that my identity is in Jesus, to be a comfort when it's easy to be consumed with your symptoms.

The Chronic Illness community is strong on social media, and on one particular day, I was scrolling and found inspiration in the quote "You are not your illness." The line might seem trite, but in that moment, I saw myself differently. It did, in a way, make me feel better. While inspirational quotes and the high you might get from it don't last more than a second, the sentiment is what I'm left with. I can't be a victim of my circumstances. In my case, my conditions came out of something genetic. I was born this way, and it's something I need to find joy and peace in. Daily, I find I have to let go of my pain and interferences because it will always be with me. Joy is something you choose. Try, instead of looking at the gloom of the hurt, to find the joy. What I'm asking of you isn't easy, I know this, but try it. See what happens. God will show up and change your heart.

Prayer

Jesus, remind me that my identity is rooted in You. When I feel reduced to my pain, whisper truth to my heart.

Prompt

List five qualities you have that have nothing to do with your illness.

Thoughts

Day 16
The World Doesn't Always Understand

But the Lord said to Samuel, "Don't judge by his appearance or height, for I have rejected him. The Lord doesn't see things the way you see them. People judge by outward appearance, but the Lord looks at the heart.

—2 Corinthians 5:17 NLT

Reflection

Invisible illness is exhausting, not just physically, but emotionally. You may look "fine," yet feel anything but. Others may misunderstand or minimize your pain. But God never does. He looks deeper, past appearances, into your true condition and your true identity. And He honors both. You don't have to convince Him. You are fully known and fully loved.

When I finally realized that I am still loved by God, then nothing else mattered. I let go of what people thought or stared at. Life looks different with chronic illness. Having the patience to learn and try something new takes courage. So take heart.

Prayer

Jesus, remind me that my identity is rooted in You. When I feel reduced to my pain, whisper truth to my heart.

Prompt

When have you felt unseen or misunderstood? What do you think God saw in that moment?

Thoughts

Day 17
Worth Isn't Measured by Productivity

Even before he made the world, God loved us and chose us in Christ to be holy and without fault in his eyes.

—Ephesians 1:4 NLT

Reflection

Our culture measures worth by output, how much you can do, produce, or achieve. Chronic illness interrupts that. But God's love was never based on your productivity. He chose you before you did a single thing. Even in rest, even in weakness, you are chosen. You are worthy because you are His.

Deadlines from work might look different for you. Asking for accommodations is never easy, but if it helps you in your daily life, don't be afraid to ask. Maybe your work life looks like asking for two days to work remotely. Or maybe it looks like working four days a week. It could also be as simple as asking for desk modifications.

What does your trust in God look like on a daily basis? If you trust him in the small things, what does trusting Him in the big things look like? Maybe it's a career shift for you or stepping back from something you've always been in charge of. Do you need to pass the proverbial baton onto someone else? This doesn't mean you are less than or not capable, but sometimes focusing on your health and well-being is more important. I've had to learn this, and every day it's scary to trust Him in His timing.

So, what do you want to ask Him in your prayers today?

Prayer

Father, help me let go of the lie that I have to earn my value. Remind me that Your love is unshakable and not performance-based.

Prompt

What do you feel pressured to "produce" or achieve to prove your worth? How might God be inviting you to let go of that?

Thoughts

Day 18
My Body, Still Holy

Don't you realize that your body is the temple of the Holy Spirit, who lives in you and was given to you by God? You do not belong to yourself.

—1 Corinthians 6:19 NLT

Reflection

When your body doesn't work the way it used to, it's tempting to see it as broken beyond use. But Scripture calls your body a temple, even in illness. Even when it aches. Even when it feels like a battleground. God's Spirit dwells within you. That means your body, as it is today, is still sacred ground.

Be gentle with your body. There might not be things you can always do after a chronic illness. It might be weaker than it once was. I learned this the hard way when I tried moving the living room coffee table with my husband. It was hard to do, and it was the first time he truly understood that things might be different from now on. I kept my pain and suffering from him for so long.

Seeing myself as a weak vessel haunted me for a long time, and I kept it from everyone. Even the partner I married. I was ashamed of who I had become, and it was difficult to understand the new person I was becoming. Sharing your hurts and how everything is changing with the person you're closest to can be the most liberating thing you can do. They care about you as much as you care for them. It took time to realize that I was still capable of doing things around the house and other tasks, but they had their own timetable. I had to once again let go of the perfectionism I was holding onto and evolve my imperfect self into a new being that was emboldened to embrace Christ and what He still had for me in my broken body.

Prayer

Holy Spirit, thank You for dwelling in this body even when it feels weak. Help me honor it, tend to it, and speak gently to it.

Prompt

Write a note of kindness or blessing to your body, acknowledging what it carries every day.

Thoughts

Day 19
Loved in the Limitation

Each time he said, "My grace is all you need. My power works best in weakness." So now I am glad to boast about my weaknesses, so that the power of Christ can work through me."

—2 Corinthians 12:9 NLT

Reflection

God didn't wait for Paul to be healed to use him. He empowered him in his weakness. The same is true for you. Your limitations don't block God's power; they become the place where His grace shines brightest. You are not less than; you are loved right here, right now, just as you are.

You are worthy in the eyes of God. At times it might not seem like it, but in the quiet moments, He's there for you. God has a plan for you, and his purpose is good.

There are days when I feel like my limitations are all that I see, and I know that's not true. When you have a job, you try to figure out ways to keep your energy levels high, but also serve your limitations. Nobody else truly understands what that is like except you. Speak up for your limitations because it matters to God. Honor your limitations and see how God honors you in it.

Prayer

Jesus, I don't like these limits. But if You meet me in them, I'll keep showing up. Let Your strength be made perfect in my weakness.

Prompt

What's one way you've seen God work through your weakness or limitation?

Thoughts

Day 20
A Story Still Being Written

And I am certain that God, who began the good work within you, will continue his work until it is finally finished on the day when Christ Jesus returns.

—Philippians 1:6 NLT

Reflection

It's easy to feel stuck in a life you didn't ask for. But your story isn't over. The God who began a good work in you is still writing, still healing, still shaping. Chronic illness may have rewritten parts of your life, but it hasn't taken the pen from God's hand. Your story is sacred because He's in it.

It's hard to predict the future, but God is in control. Worrying about what might come serves no purpose. I recently had to come to terms with the fact that worrying will not truly get you anywhere. It was after a week of being sick and then celebrating my fifth wedding anniversary. I wanted to be happy and excited, as usual, but I couldn't bring myself to be. A new symptom had been filling me with dread, and there was nothing I could do about it. Finally, after admitting it to my husband, I hadn't been myself, I told God I'd let the feeling go. The anxiety and fear of what if plagued me, and it was time to let it be. Soon enough, I'd find an answer, but fretting over it wasn't going to be a solution. God still had good work for me to do, regardless of a new illness or diagnosis.

Prayer

Lord, even when I feel unfinished or forgotten, help me trust that You're still at work. I give You the pen again today.

Prompt

What "chapters" of your life feel disrupted by illness? What new ones might God be writing?

Thoughts

Day 21
Beloved. Period.

See how very much our Father loves us, for he calls us his children, and that is what we are!

—1 John 3:1a NLT

Reflection

No condition, no diagnosis, no limitation can change the fact that you are beloved. Not because of what you can do. Not in spite of your illness. But simply because you are God's child. That truth remains, even when everything else feels unstable. You are broken and beloved. Both. At the same time.

Admitting you need help can be difficult. God wants all of you, even in your imperfections. Each year, I learned how to manage my illnesses better to get stronger, but it's easy to forget I was beloved. You are worthy of God's love every second of every day. Recently, I realized I needed to get creative with balancing a full-time job, and it was difficult to come to terms with this. I'm so used to working too many hours, but now scaling back seems like I'm finally honoring myself. There's a peace I can only get from God alone. Where do you need to scale back? Is it in your personal, professional, or spiritual life?

Prayer

God, thank you for loving me completely and unconditionally. Let that truth steady me when I forget who I am.

Prompt

Finish this sentence: "Even though I'm struggling with _____, I am still deeply loved by God because _____."

Thoughts

Week 4 Hope That Holds On

Theme Verse: "For I know the plans I have for you," says the Lord. "They are plans for good and not for disaster, to give you a future and a hope."
—Jeremiah 29:11 NLT

Even when your present feels uncertain, God's hope secures your future.

Day 22
Holding on to Hope

Let us hold tightly without wavering to the hope we affirm, for God can be trusted to keep his promise.

—Hebrews 10:23 NLT

Reflection

Hope feels fragile when pain is constant. But Hebrews encourages us to grasp hope with a firm grip, because God never breaks His promises. Your hope isn't wishful thinking; it's a confident expectation based on God's faithfulness. When the fog of illness clouds your path, hold on tight. God's promises are the anchor that won't let you drift.

Does God seem distant to you right now? When I moved to a new state yet again, chasing something I thought was right for me, God felt distant. Transition can be a challenging time when everything seems new and unfamiliar. When I moved back to the West, the culture passed me by, and I knew it was there, but I didn't adjust well to it. My husband and I church-hopped, feeling one out and finally leaving after a while. We were so used to not being accepted that we might not have felt we belonged anywhere, and moving to this new city was a mistake. God didn't seem to be opening any doors, and it was frustrating. Of course, looking back, it's easy to see that God was listening, but in another way. Finally, after years of living in the new city, we found a different kind of church body. On the first Sunday, I broke down in tears in front of the pastor's wife. It was the first time in months that I had heard from the Lord in a clear voice. I never gave up hope of hearing God's voice, but it was dim and in the background turned down low. It's not even that the sermon was life-changing; I don't even know what it was about anymore, but it was about the people. The church body was accepting and warm. They weren't into optics or trying to present in a certain way. They were there because they loved and heard from God. Surround yourself with God-fearing people, and you will find the volume turns up to listen to His voice.

Prayer

God, when I feel like letting go, remind me that You are faithful and worthy of my hope. Help me hold on.

Prompt

What promises of God have helped you hold on during difficult days?

Thoughts

Day 23
Strength for Today

The Lord gives his people strength. The Lord blesses them with peace.

—Psalm 29:11 NLT

Reflection

Some days, just getting through feels overwhelming. Psalm 29 reminds us that God's strength is available now, right where you are. It's not distant or delayed. And with strength comes peace. You don't have to carry the weight alone. God's strength empowers your weak moments and brings calm to your restless heart.

The city I live in has days that are extremely hot and days that are temperate. I used to be an avid hiker in my early twenties, but I'm not as much now. There's a grief that comes with feeling as though you're shut in or trapped in your house. On days I am able to get outside and see the environment, I pray to God to give me strength to do so. Even if I'm tired the next day, it's worth it to keep doing the things I love.

If I worship, then I hear the voice of the Lord give me strength to do all things. Knowing this psalm exists gives anyone the courage to find peace in their circumstances.

Consider this prayer to meditate on in your prayer time

Ascribe to the Lord Glory
A Psalm of David.
29 Ascribe to the Lord, O heavenly beings, [a]
I ascribe to the Lord glory and strength.
2 Ascribe to the Lord the glory due his name;
worship the Lord in the splendor of holiness. [b]

3 The voice of the Lord is over the waters;
the God of glory thunders,
the Lord, over many waters.
4 The voice of the Lord is powerful;
the voice of the Lord is full of majesty.
5 The voice of the Lord breaks the cedars;
the Lord breaks the cedars of Lebanon.
6 He makes Lebanon to skip like a calf,
and Sirion like a young wild ox.
7 The voice of the Lord flashes forth flames of fire.
8 The voice of the Lord shakes the wilderness;
the Lord shakes the wilderness of Kadesh.
9 The voice of the Lord makes the deer give birth[c]
and strips the forests bare,
and in his temple all cry, "Glory!"
10 The Lord sits enthroned over the flood;
the Lord sits enthroned as king forever.
11 May the Lord give strength to his people!
May the Lord bless[d] his people with peace!

—Psalm 29:1-11

Prayer

Lord, fill me with Your strength today. Help me rest in Your peace, even when my body struggles.

Prompt

Recall a moment when God's strength or peace lifted you unexpectedly. How can you lean into that memory today?

Thoughts

Day 24
Trusting God's Timing

He has made everything beautiful in its time.

—Ecclesiastes 3:11a NLT

Reflection

Waiting is one of the hardest parts of chronic illness, waiting for healing, relief, or clarity. Ecclesiastes reminds us that God's timing is perfect, even when it feels slow or confusing. The beauty of your story is still unfolding. Trust that God is weaving every moment, even the painful ones, into something good and beautiful.

Waiting to get test results is sometimes the most challenging time in a chronic illness. You're waiting on other people to do their jobs, since your sample is in a queue of hundreds. Whether it's good, bad, or neutral news, it's a step in the right direction. While most of the time, test results tell you nothing is wrong, and you're perfectly "healthy," that is still a message. I find I draw closer to God in the waiting. I want so desperately to know immediately. This world has programmed us to want it now and faster, but that's not how lab testing works. Here's to you, who is waiting on that result, whatever the outcome. I hope you wait well in the mystery that lies ahead.

There was a six-month period where I was waiting to see if a biopsy had turned out to be cancer or not. It was an incredibly stressful period because there was a chance it could actually be cancer. This was the first time something serious could've happened. At this time, I wrestled with God and tried not to despair. Everyone around you has something, but it still feels lonely. I had two procedures to remove the precancer, and thankfully, after that, the results were positive. The call was, "The margin is clear, and you're healthy." The relief that washed over me was joy. When I was in it, I didn't know how stressed I was. It was as if the world became a little more beautiful. How do you trust God in his timing?

Prayer

God, help me trust Your timing, even when I want answers now. Let me rest in Your perfect plan.

Prompt

What areas of your health or life do you find hardest to wait on? How might God be working in that waiting?

Thoughts

Day 25
Trusting God's Timing

Two people are better off than one... If either of them falls down, one can help the other up.

—Ecclesiastes 4:9-10a NLT

Reflection

Chronic illness can be isolating, but God designed us for connection. Leaning on others is not a weakness; it's a sign of wisdom. Whether a friend, family member, or part of a community of believers, we need one another. When you're weak, someone else's strength can lift you. And you, in turn, can be a strength for another.

I have found that social media offers the biggest community for chronic illness. Bigger than my own church body, and I've leaned on the chronic illness community for advice, support, and laughs. Some of my most interesting relationships have developed with people I've met on social media. When you find a fellow spoonie that gets you, then you have a kindred spirit. It doesn't matter the age or condition, we have a common vocabulary. It's easier to lift one up in the community when this happens. It's hard at times to find that in a church body. There are usually no groups that meet specifically for the chronically ill. Although I attended one church that offered Soul Care and a group for the chronically ill, it was truly incredible. It was worth the drive across town for at least a little while. I hope you find your community if you're still searching for it, friend. Chronic illness is terrible to move through alone. Even if you have to educate your current community on your condition, if you put in the work, it can work out for the better. You might lose others along the way, but not everyone will go. Some will show up in ways you never knew possible. If you're able, try to create a group at your church. You can find fellow believers who are fellow Spoonies to surround yourself with support.

If you want to be a prayer warrior on social media, there are a variety of ways to make an impact for the chronic illness community.

- Share honest encouragement instead of perfection.
- Offer short prayers for others.
- Share comforting scripture or uplifting thoughts.
- Use your story to reassure others they are not alone.
- Post gentle reminders to drink water, rest, stretch, or take meds
- Ask your audience how you can pray for them.
- Share small victories, like completing simple daily tasks.
- Celebrate disabled joy and moments of peace or gratitude.
- Validate hard days with kind words.
- Post about rest and self care as something holy and necessary.
- Share resources for accessible worship, like audio Bibles or captioned sermons.
- Normalize mobility aids and accommodations.
- Offer "save this for later" comfort posts.
- Speak blessings over your community.
- Share gratitude lists highlighting small, meaningful moments.
- Use humor lightly and kindly to connect.
- Post reflections about God's presence in quiet places.
- Remind people of their worth outside productivity.
- Encourage boundaries and modeling rest without guilt.

Prayer

Jesus, help me to both receive and offer support in community. Let Your love flow through these relationships.

Prompt

Who in your life encourages you? How might you reach out to them this week?

Thoughts

Day 26
Light in the Darkness

The light shines in the darkness, and the darkness can never extinguish it.

—John 1:5 NLT

Reflection

Illness often feels like a heavy shadow, but God's light shines even brighter in the darkest places. This light is not just physical healing, but the hope, love, and peace God brings into your soul. No matter how deep the darkness feels today, God's light is greater, and it will never be overcome.

14 You are the light of the world—like a city on a hilltop that cannot be hidden. 15 No one lights a lamp and then puts it under a basket. Instead, a lamp is placed on a stand, where it gives light to everyone in the house. 16 In the same way, let your good deeds shine out for all to see, so that everyone will praise your heavenly Father.
—Matthew 5:14–16 NLT

This scripture comes to mind when talking of darkness. Coming back to the idea of shining light in dark places is important. Sharing your faith and recounting your story of perseverance through difficult times is a source of hope for others. Now, I'm not saying your existence is meant to inspire others. I do know that others find your story to be a source of hope when they have days of struggle. You're a reminder that God hasn't forgotten them, because you were loved even in the face of your diagnosis. Even if you are never healed from your disease or condition, God shines His eternal light over you every day. People can tell a difference in you.

The year the song "Way Maker" came out is what I always think of when I'm seeking light in the darkness. I first heard it at a Passion conference, and it made me feel closer to God. Do you have a worship song that makes you move closer to Him?

There's so much darkness in the chronic illness space, and being there to pray and lift others up is important. I never knew that God would give me a specific group of people to minister to when I was younger. I did have a particular group of people of another religion I would pray for before I got sick, but now I know that was God preparing me for the chronic illness community. What community has your heart to pray and lift up?

Prayer

Lord, shine Your light into the dark places of my life. Help me see Your presence when all feels dim.

Prompt

Write about a time when you felt God's light during a dark season.

Thoughts

Day 27
Perseverance Through Pain

We are pressed on every side by troubles, but we are not crushed.

—2 Corinthians 4:8 NLT

Reflection

Pain presses hard, yet God's grace keeps you from being crushed. Your perseverance is testimony to His sustaining power. Even when your body feels weak, your spirit can remain strong. God carries you through every hardship, not by immediately removing the pressure, but by holding you steady beneath it.

At the beginning of every fall, I always have to use my cane to acclimate back into walking more. It's on those days that I look to God for help to keep going and walking. The heat also makes it harder to walk through, but eventually my legs and knees get used to the activity again, and I keep going. It takes courage to use my cane at times, because it's a part of me that's new to others. I have to figure out how much or little I will say to anyone about it. In the moment when someone asks, I decide whether to share. It isn't usually their business to know why you have to use a mobility aid, or the invisible conditions you have, but people don't usually mean to offend. At times, I take the moment to educate because my condition is not visible or well-known enough. You don't have to tell anyone about your condition, but what if God has given you an opportunity to share about your faith through the pain? It could be a way for the other person to be interested in your story, and a way to talk about how God has given you the strength every day to keep going. Don't make it about why you need a mobility device or why you're exhausted; make it about the positive of being a witness to Christ's love and provision.

Prayer

God, when I feel overwhelmed, remind me that You are my strength. Help me persevere today, trusting in Your power.

Prompt

What helps you keep going when pain or fatigue threatens to overwhelm? How do you respond when others want to know why you're feeling the way you do?

Thoughts

Day 28
Restoring Joy

You have turned my mourning into joyful dancing.

—Psalm 30:11a NLT

Reflection

There will be moments of mourning, losses you grieve deeply. But God promises restoration. Joy can return, even after long seasons of pain. Your story is filled with laughter, celebration, and hope. Hold onto that promise when joy feels far away.

For a time, I visited physical therapy frequently. There was a month when my hips, legs, and knees were in so much pain I didn't know if it would ever go away. I thought, well, this is it. I am going to have to grieve my life as I know it, and this is now my new normal. After I let those thoughts go and gave them to God, I felt joy return to my life. Eventually, my strength returned, and that brief period of pain subsided, but I was ready for that change if it did happen. Sometimes, saying the fear out loud is a way of acceptance and then giving it to God.

Prayer

Lord, bring joy into the places that feel broken and heavy. Help me dance again in Your freedom.

Prompt

What brings you joy today? How can you nurture that spark, even on difficult days?

Thoughts

Day 29
God's Ever-Present Help

You have turned my mourning into joyful dancing.

—Psalm 30:11a NLT

Reflection

No matter what tomorrow brings, God is your refuge. When the storms rage inside or outside, He is your shelter and your strength. You are never alone or forgotten. This truth can anchor you through every struggle.

Even when you don't know what to pray for, ask God to open your heart to hear His Spirit. Ask him for wisdom or grace. Perhaps asking God for help or praying for someone to be more open to your condition is worth considering. God answers prayers, even when it's not in your timing.

I am a filmmaker when I'm not writing, and when I was making my last documentary about the chronic illness I had, there were times I wanted to give up. It took a lot of praying and support from others to keep making the film. Even when I didn't think I had a story and everything was going wrong, "for the record, it wasn't, but in my head it was," I prayed to God to help me find the path through. Every person I interviewed gave me the confidence to also keep going. They told me that this will help gain awareness of Hypermobile Ehlers-Danlos Syndrome, and they thanked me for doing this work. The interviewees never knew how close I was to giving up every time I met with someone new. Each time, they reminded me I had to keep going. God kept opening doors for the film, and while I didn't get it done in my time or my producer's time, it was finished in His perfect timing.

Prayer

God, thank You for being my refuge. Help me run to You whenever I feel overwhelmed.

Prompt

How can you remind yourself daily that God is your refuge and strength?

Thoughts

Day 30
A Hopeful Future

You will fill me with joy in your presence, with eternal pleasures at your right hand.

—Psalm 16:11b NLT

Reflection

Your present may be filled with uncertainty, but your future with God is certain and full of joy. The hope you hold on to is not just for this life, but for eternity. Rest in that promise today and every day.

When I think about the future of my illnesses, I am filled with hope. There are incredible scientists working every day to raise awareness and develop therapies to manage symptoms. One day, there will be a new classification system to identify my rare condition, so hopefully it won't be as invisible as it is now. So many people have my condition, but it's so rarely talked about. My hope is that the condition will be as common as other conditions like diabetes or MS. With my work on my documentary and others telling their stories through film, I hope it raises awareness of the condition.

While you're not guaranteed tomorrow, or next week, or the year, choose God with all your hope and strength. Symptoms come and go, and at times are so erratic that it's confusing. I hope you have hope that God will be with you at every step.

And if you have never allowed Jesus into your heart, today is the day to do it. All you need to do is ask Jesus to forgive you of your sins and believe that He is the son of God. He is there for you and loves you every minute of every second.

What step do you need to take today?

Prayer

Lord, thank You for the hope of eternal joy with You. Help me live each day in the light of that hope.

Prompt

Write a letter to your future self, reminding them of God's hope and faithfulness.

Thoughts

Glossary of Chronic Illness
and Invisible Illness Terms

Ableism
Bias or discrimination toward disabled people, often based on assumptions about what a body or mind "should" be able to do.

Access Needs
The support a person requires to participate fully in life, including rest breaks, quiet spaces, flexible schedules, or communication tools.

Accommodations
Specific adjustments that help someone function safely and comfortably, such as extended deadlines, seating options, or mobility support.

Baseline
A person's usual level of functioning when symptoms are stable.

Brain Fog
Difficulty concentrating, remembering, or thinking clearly due to pain, fatigue, medication effects, or neurological issues.

Care Fatigue
The exhaustion that comes from managing appointments, insurance, symptoms, and daily medical responsibilities.

Chronic Illness
A long term health condition that affects daily life. Symptoms may be constant or fluctuate.

Crash
A sudden loss of energy or ability after pushing beyond one's limits.

Crip Time
A concept that recognizes disabled people often move through time differently because of pain levels, fatigue, or medical needs.

Disabled Joy
Moments of delight, strength, or peace within disabled life, resisting the belief that disability is only hardship.

Dynamic Disability
A disability that changes from day to day. Some days a person can do more, other days far less.

Flare or Flare Up
A period of increased symptoms beyond the usual baseline.

Invisible Illness
A health condition that affects someone deeply yet is not visible from the outside.

Masking
Downplaying or hiding symptoms in order to function socially or meet expectations.

Medical Gaslighting
When a healthcare professional dismisses or doubts a patient's symptoms, often blaming them on anxiety or exaggeration.

Medical Trauma
Emotional or psychological pain that develops from negative healthcare experiences or repeated dismissal.

Mobility Aid
Any device that helps a person move with comfort and safety, such as canes, rollators, wheelchairs, or braces.

Mobility Aid User
Someone who regularly or occasionally uses mobility aids, even if they can sometimes walk without them.

Pain Scale
A tool for describing pain intensity. People often say "my ten is not your ten" because pain is personal and subjective.

Pacing
Managing energy by breaking activities into smaller steps with rest between tasks.

PEM (Post Exertional Malaise)
A delayed worsening of symptoms after physical, mental, or emotional activity.

Spoon Theory
A metaphor that compares energy to spoons. Daily tasks cost spoons, and people with chronic illness have fewer spoons to spend.

Spoonie
A person who lives with chronic or invisible illness and uses Spoon Theory to describe their energy.

Weather Sensitivity
A symptom pattern where changes in temperature, humidity, or pressure increase pain or fatigue.

Zebra
A symbol used by people with Ehlers Danlos Syndrome, honoring the idea that sometimes the uncommon diagnosis is the correct one.

A Devotional Reflection
on the Colors of Disability Pride

Black: In Memory and in Mercy

The black of the flag reminds us of the lives lost to injustice and neglect. Yet in Scripture, black is also the color before creation, the deep place where God speaks light into being. When we sit in the quiet shadows of pain or exhaustion, God meets us there. Nothing about our suffering is unseen. The Spirit stays close to those who are worn and waiting, and light rises gently from the dark.

Prayer

God, rest with me in the shadows. Let your presence surround every memory of harm. Bring healing to places that still ache.

Red: Strength in the Body You Gave Me

Red stands for physical disability. It reminds us of blood that carries life. It also reminds us that Jesus lived in a human body that grew tired, that held pain, that required rest. There is holiness in the body you have, not in the one the world tells you to wish for. God is not disappointed by your limits. God dwells there.

Prayer

Lord, bless this body. Teach me to honor it. Help me feel your love through the strength you give for each day.

Gold: The Light of Neurodiversity

Gold shines on the beauty of minds that process the world in ways that are quiet, brilliant, tender, or simply different. God's creativity flourishes in the diversity of thought and emotion. You do not need to fit a mold to be precious. Your presence adds color to the world.

Prayer

God of wisdom, thank you for the way you shaped my mind. Let me see its value and walk in the beauty of your design.

White: The Hidden Stories of Invisible Illness

White represents chronic illness and conditions that others cannot see. It is the color of manna, the hidden sustenance God provided in the wilderness. When the world does not understand our pain, God understands. God gives strength in quiet ways, grace that falls like small mercies each morning.

Prayer

Lord, be my daily bread. Provide what I need when others cannot see my need. Let your presence be enough for today.

Blue: The Deep Waters of Mental Health

Blue holds the depth of emotion and the storms of the mind. It reminds us of the God who walks on water and calms waves with a word. Your emotions are not failures. Your mind is not too heavy for God to carry. Even in the deep waters, you are held.

Prayer

God of peace, steady my thoughts. Sit with me in the waters and speak calm into my spirit.

Green: The Sensory World Where God Meets Us

Green represents sensory disabilities and the many ways people experience the world. It evokes pastures and still places where God invites us to lie down and rest. Sensory experiences can overwhelm or soothe, but through them we learn to listen for God's gentleness.

Prayer

Shepherd of my soul, guide me to restful pastures. Help me honor my senses and find comfort in your presence.

The Diagonal Stroke: Moving Forward with God

The sweeping line across the flag reminds us that disability is not stillness. It is movement, adaptation, resilience. It is the testimony that life with chronic illness continues with intention and courage. The line is not straight, yet it moves with purpose. So do you. God walks the uneven path beside you.

Prayer

God of the onward journey, walk with me. Give me courage for each step, grace for each limit, and strength for each tomorrow.

Definition Reflections and Scripture

Scripture

Thank you for making me so wonderfully complex! Your workmanship is marvelous—how well I know it. Psalm 139:14 NLT

Reflection Question

Where have I felt pressure to meet standards that were never meant for my body or my life?

Scripture

Share each other's burdens, and in this way obey the law of Christ. Galatians 6:2 NLT

Reflection Question

How can I honor my access needs without apologizing for them?

Scripture

The Lord helps the fallen and lifts those bent beneath their loads. Psalm 145:14 NLT

Reflection Question

What is one accommodation that allows me to live with more peace, and how can I embrace it with gratitude?

Scripture

Each time he said, "My grace is all you need. My power works best in weakness." So now I am glad to boast about my weaknesses, so that the power of Christ can work through me. 2 Corinthians 12:9 Psalm 139:14 NLT

Reflection Question

How can I be more compassionate with myself when my baseline shifts?

Scripture

For the Lord grants wisdom! From his mouth came knowledge and understanding. Proverbs 2:6 NLT

Reflection Question

What helps me slow down and offer myself grace when my mind feels heavy or unclear?

Scripture

Then Jesus said, "Come to me, all of you who are weary and carry heavy burdens, and I will give you rest." Matthew 11:28 NLT

Reflection Question

Where can I invite rest into the parts of my life that feel overmanaged or overwhelmed?

Scripture

The Lord is close to the brokenhearted; he rescues those whose spirits are crushed. Psalm 34:18 NLT

Reflection Question

How have my challenges shaped my faith, resilience, or compassion for others?

Scripture

He renews my strength. He guides me along the right paths, bringing honor to his name. Psalm 23:3 NLT

Reflection Question

What signs can I look for that tell me I need to pause before I reach a crash point?

Scripture

For everything there is a season, a time for every activity under heaven. Ecclesiastes 3:1 NLT

Reflection Question

How can I embrace a slower rhythm without comparing myself to others?

Scripture

This is the day the Lord has made. We will rejoice and be glad in it. Psalm 118:24 NLT

Reflection Question

Where have I found joy in unexpected places, and how can I nurture more of it?

Scripture

The faithful love of the Lord never ends! [a] His mercies never cease. Lamentations 3:22 NLT

Reflection Question

How can I give myself permission to have different limits on different days?

Scripture

But when I am afraid, I will put my trust in you. Psalm 56:3 NLT

Reflection Question

What comforts or routines help me when my symptoms increase?

Scripture

But the Lord said to Samuel, "Don't judge by his appearance or height, for I have rejected him. The Lord doesn't see things the way you see them. People judge by outward appearance, but the Lord looks at the heart." 1 Samuel 16:7 NLT

Reflection Question

In what ways can I validate my own experiences even when others cannot see them?

Scripture

The Lord is close to all who call on him, yes, to all who call on him in truth. Psalm 145:18 NLT

Reflection Question

Where am I still trying to appear fine, and how can I create safe spaces to be honest?

Scripture

Do not be afraid or discouraged, for the Lord will personally go ahead of you. He will be with you; he will neither fail you nor abandon you. Deuteronomy 31:8 NLT

Reflection Question

How can I remind myself that my symptoms and experiences are real even when others doubt them?

Scripture

For the angel of the Lord is a guard; he surrounds and defends all who fear him. Psalm 34:7 NLT

Reflection Question

What gentle practices help me feel safe again in medical settings?

Scripture

The Lord is my strength and shield. I trust him with all my heart. He helps me, and my heart is filled with joy. I burst out in songs of thanksgiving. Psalm 28:7 NLT

Reflection Question

How can I view my mobility supports as tools of provision rather than signs of limitation?

Scripture

I will be your God throughout your lifetime— until your hair is white with age. I made you, and I will care for you. I will carry you along and save you. Isaiah 46:4 NLT

Reflection Question

What freedom or relief do my mobility aids give me that I want to acknowledge today?

Scripture

You keep track of all my sorrows. [a]
You have collected all my tears in your bottle.
You have recorded each one in your book.
Psalm 56:8 NLT

Reflection Question

How can I better communicate my pain in ways that feel truthful and honoring to myself?

Scripture

Be still, and know that I am God. Psalm 46:10 NLT

Reflection Question

What boundaries or rhythms help me maintain my energy without guilt?

Scripture

But those who trust in the Lord will find new strenght. They will soar high on wings like eagles. They will run and not grow weary. They will walk and not faint. Isaiah 40:31 NLT

Reflection Question
How can I prepare for recovery time after meaningful but draining activities?

Scripture
My health may fail, and my spirit may grow weak, but God remains the strength of my heart; he is mine forever. Psalm 73:26 NLT

Reflection Question
What tasks or responsibilities are costing more spoons than I can afford right now?

Scripture
Give your burdens to the Lord, and he will take care of you. He will not permit the godly to slip and fall.   Psalm 55:22 NLT

Reflection Question
How can I ask for help or support when my spoons are low?

Scripture
He calmed the storm to a whisper and stilled the waves. Psalm 107:29 NLT

Reflection Question
What comforts or adjustments help me on days when the weather affects my body?

Scripture
Thank you for making me so wonderfully complex! Your workmanship is marvelous—how well I know it. Psalm 139:14 NLT

Reflection Question
How has my uniqueness made me stronger, wiser, or more compassionate?

Acknowledgements

This book wouldn't have been possible without the Holy Spirit's kindness prompting me to put my thoughts on the page. I struggled for many years with imposter syndrome. At the end of the day, it's my shared experiences that hopefully made you feel less alone.

To my amazing husband, Marshall, who is always so supportive in all of my creative endeavors. Thank you for pushing me to grow closer to God. Your spiritual leadership gave me the courage even to try.

To Angela, without you, this book would be the shell of what it is today. I love your kind words, questions, and thoughts on each day you wrote about. You also gave me many topics to think about and explore further. Your thoughts made me feel that being vulnerable was necessary, even if it was scary.

To Tiara, while you and I have never met in person, your thoughts live on through the feedback on these pages. You're the internet friend who made me feel less alone on days when it was hard. The person who was always telling people you would pray for them. You're a sweet soul, and I am so grateful to you.

To Elizabeth, without seeing you open your bible and tell everyone why you care about getting into the Word, I wouldn't have been inspired to write and share my story. The simple images you posted online gave me the courage to write this devotional. The faith you have in God gives me strength to keep following Him.

To Emma, who kept me accountable throughout the writing of this book. You asked about it, and I wanted to keep going. So often in a creative endeavor, there are points where I feel like giving up, and at that exact moment, someone reminds me to keep going. Thank you for being the motivator I needed.

About the Author

Jennifer Kain is a filmmaker, writer, and advocate dedicated to telling stories that inspire empathy and change. With a heart for advocacy, her work focuses on disability and faith. She believes storytelling is a powerful tool for connection, healing, and awareness, and she uses her creative platforms to encourage honesty, dignity, and hope. You can find out more about her at jenniferkain.me

www.ingramcontent.com/pod-product-compliance
Lightning Source LLC
Chambersburg PA
CBHW051633120626
46551CB00014B/2060